OVERCOMING *Anxiety*

ONE SCRIPTURE AT A TIME

30-DAY JOURNAL

This journal belongs to:

_____

Watersprings
PUBLISHING

Overcoming Anxiety, One Scripture at a Time

Published by Watersprings Media House, LLC.

P.O. Box 1284

Olive Branch, MS 38654

www.waterspringsmedia.com

© 2018 Copyrights Watersprings Media House. All rights reserved.

No portion of this book may be reproduced, stored in a retrieval system or transmitted in any form or by any means (electronic, mechanical, photocopy, recording, scanning, or other), except for brief quotations in critical reviews of articles, without the prior written permission of the writer.

Scripture quotations credited to NIV are from the Holy Bible, New International Version. Copyright © 1973, 1978, 1984, 2011 by Biblica, Inc. Used by permission. All rights reserved worldwide.

ISBN 13: 978-1-948877-14-5

Introduction

Researchers say that one in three adults will experience some type of anxiety disorder at some point in their life. If you happen to be one of those people, there is hope and healing; and it can be found in the Word of God. In the early summer of 2017, I began to experience chest pains and shortness of breath that eventually led to me spending hours in the ER, the doctor's office and undergoing a series of tests. Each test came back with positive outcomes and the concluded diagnosis was stress and anxiety. Of the many ways anxiety can manifest itself, for me it was in the form of cardiovascular issues. Once I realized what was going on, I was determined to not let anxiety cripple my life and impede my purpose. I became more intentional about my eating and exercise habits, and most importantly, I sought out the Word of God.

How to Use this Scripture Writing Journal

Over the next 30 days you will meditate on many of the same scriptures that helped me to overcome anxiety. It is my hope and prayer that through this journal you too will have victory over anxiety, one scripture at a time. This journal provides four sections a day to write from the provided scripture:

Write - As you write the Word of God, allow it to penetrate your heart and mind afresh, even if it is a familiar scripture.

Listen - Listen to your heart, good, bad or indifferent and simply write. Then listen to the heart of God through that scripture and/or in that moment and write what you hear or what you understand from that scripture.

Pray - Next, take a moment to reconcile your heart and thoughts with God's words, then write a prayer from your heart. Acknowledge who God is and where you are, thanking and asking God for what you need in that moment.

My Affirmation - At the end of each entry write a personal affirmation. Take it a step further, put it on a post-it note, your cell phone screen, or make it your daily hashtag on social media. Speak it, and repeat it until you feel a difference in your spirit.

LeWinfred A. Shack

#IAMFREE

Do not be anxious about anything, but in every situation, by prayer and petition, with thanksgiving, present your requests to God. And the peace of God, which transcends all understanding, will guard your hearts and your minds in Christ Jesus.

Philippians 4:6-7

Write the Word

Listen to the Word

Pray the Word

My Affirmation:

"Come to me, all you who are weary and burdened, and I will give you rest. Take my yoke upon you and learn from me, for I am gentle and humble in heart, and you will find rest for your souls. For my yoke is easy and my burden is light."

Matthew 11:28-30

Write the Word

Listen to the Word

Pray the Word

My Affirmation:

Peace I leave with you; my peace I give you. I do not give to you as the world gives. Do not let your hearts be troubled and do not be afraid.

John 14:27

Write the Word

Listen to the Word

Pray the Word

My Affirmation:

Let the peace of Christ rule in your hearts, since as members of one body you were called to peace. And be thankful.

Colossians 3:15

Write the Word

Listen to the Word

Pray the Word

My Affirmation:

Cast your cares on the Lord and he will sustain you; he will never let the righteous be shaken.

Psalm 55:22

Write the Word

Listen to the Word

Pray the Word

My Affirmation:

Why, my soul, are you downcast? Why so disturbed within me? Put your hope in God, for I will yet praise him, my Savior and my God.

Psalm 42:5

Write the Word

Listen to the Word

Pray the Word

My Affirmation:

Anxiety weighs down the heart, but a kind word cheers it up.

Proverbs 12:25

Write the Word

Listen to the Word

Pray the Word

My Affirmation:

So we say with confidence, "The Lord is my helper, I will not be afraid. What can man do to me?"

Hebrews 13:6

Write the Word

Listen to the Word

Pray the Word

My Affirmation:

When I am afraid, I put my trust in you. In God, whose word I praise -- in God I trust and am not afraid. What can mere mortals do to me?

Psalm 56:3-4

Write the Word

Listen to the Word

Pray the Word

My Affirmation:

Trust in the Lord with all your heart and lean not on your own understanding; in all your ways submit to him, and he will make your paths straight.

Proverbs 3:5-6

Write the Word

Listen to the Word

Pray the Word

My Affirmation:

For I am convinced that neither death nor life, neither angels nor demons, neither the present nor the future, nor any powers, neither height nor depth, nor anything else in all creation, will be able to separate us from the love of God that is in Christ Jesus our Lord.

Romans 8:38-39

Write the Word

Listen to the Word

Pray the Word

My Affirmation:

"Abba, Father," he said, "everything is possible for you. Take this cup from me. Yet not what I will, but what you will."

Mark 14:36

Write the Word

Listen to the Word

Pray the Word

My Affirmation:

I was young and now I am old, yet I have never seen the righteous forsaken or their children begging bread.

Psalm 37:25

Write the Word

Listen to the Word

Pray the Word

My Affirmation:

No temptation has overtaken you except what is common to mankind. And God is faithful; he will not let you be tempted beyond what you can bear. But when you are tempted, he will also provide a way out so that you can endure it.

1 Corinthians 10:13

Write the Word

Listen to the Word

Pray the Word

My Affirmation:

Have I not commanded you? Be strong and courageous. Do not be afraid; do not be discouraged, for the Lord your God will be with you wherever you go."

Joshua 1:9

Write the Word

Listen to the Word

Pray the Word

My Affirmation:

Do not be afraid, you worm Jacob, little Israel, do not fear, for I myself will help you," declares the Lord, your Redeemer, the Holy One of Israel.

Isaiah 41:14

Write the Word

Listen to the Word

Pray the Word

My Affirmation:

Not only so, but we also glory in our sufferings, because we know that suffering produces perseverance; perseverance, character; and character, hope. And hope does not put us to shame, because God's love has been poured out into our hearts through the Holy Spirit, who has been given to us.

Romans 5:3-5

Write the Word

Listen to the Word

Pray the Word

My Affirmation:

*When I said, "My foot is slipping,"
your unfailing love, Lord, supported me.
When anxiety was great within me, your
consolation brought me joy.*

Psalm 94:18-19

Write the Word

Listen to the Word

Pray the Word

My Affirmation:

Consider it pure joy, my brothers and sisters, whenever you face trials of many kinds, because you know that the testing of your faith produces perseverance. Let perseverance finish its work so that you may be mature and complete, not lacking anything.

James 1:2-4

Write the Word

Listen to the Word

Pray the Word

My Affirmation:

*"For I know the plans I have for you,"
declares the Lord , "plans to prosper you
and not to harm you, plans to give you
hope and a future.*

Jeremiah 29:11

Write the Word

Listen to the Word

Pray the Word

My Affirmation:

Even youths grow tired and weary, and young men stumble and fall; but those who hope in the Lord will renew their strength. They will soar on wings like eagles; they will run and not grow weary, they will walk and not be faint.

Isaiah 40:30-31

Write the Word

Listen to the Word

Pray the Word

My Affirmation:

Now faith is confidence in what we hope for and assurance about what we do not see.

Hebrews 11:1

Write the Word

Listen to the Word

Pray the Word

My Affirmation:

May the God of hope fill you with all joy and peace as you trust in him, so that you may overflow with hope by the power of the Holy Spirit.

Romans 15:13

Write the Word

Listen to the Word

Pray the Word

My Affirmation:

"Consider how the wild flowers grow. They do not labor or spin. Yet I tell you, not even Solomon in all his splendor was dressed like one of these. If that is how God clothes the grass of the field, which is here today, and tomorrow is thrown into the fire, how much more will he clothe you—you of little faith!

Luke 12:27-28

Write the Word

Listen TO THE WORD

Pray the Word

My Affirmation:

Do not be anxious about anything, but in every situation, by prayer and petition, with thanksgiving, present your requests to God. And the peace of God, which transcends all understanding, will guard your hearts and your minds in Christ Jesus.

Philippians 4:6-7

Write the Word

Listen to the Word

Pray the Word

My Affirmation:

Cast all your anxiety on him because he cares for you.

1 Peter 5:7

Write the Word

Listen to the Word

Pray the Word

My Affirmation:

Keep your lives free from the love of money and be content with what you have, because God has said, "Never will I leave you; never will I forsake you."

Hebrews 13:5

Write the Word

Listen to the Word

Pray the Word

My Affirmation:

No, in all these things we are more than conquerors through him who loved us.

Romans 8:37

Write the Word

Listen to the Word

Pray the Word

My Affirmation:

David was greatly distressed because the men were talking of stoning him; each one was bitter in spirit because of his sons and daughters. But David found strength in the Lord his God.

1 Samuel 30:6

Write the Word

Listen to the Word

Pray the Word

My Affirmation:

Now may the Lord of peace himself give you peace at all times and in every way. The Lord be with all of you.

2 Thessalonians 3:16

Write the Word

Listen to the Word

Pray the Word

My Affirmation:

MORE JOURNALS

www.WriteListenPray.com

www.ingramcontent.com/pod-product-compliance
Lightning Source LLC
Chambersburg PA
CBHW060046230426
43661CB00004B/674